Before You Begin

This isn't a guide.

There's nothing here to follow.

No steps. No safety net. Just fragments of truth, sharpened into something you might not want to hold.

You won't find clarity in every page.

Sometimes you'll only find a mirror, and even that will feel like a threat.

The words are simple. The damage is not.

Sit with what stings.

Ignore what flatters.

And read as if something inside you needs to be disturbed

I
THE MASKS
WE WEAR

At first, the mask hides you.
Then it replaces you.

The line between sinner and saint is drawn by law, not by conscience.

We mistake legality for morality, because it's easier to outsource judgement than confront our own values.

But laws are scaffolding built by flawed hands, not divine lines etched into reality.

A saint in one system is a criminal in another. So, what does that make righteousness, other than branding?

In truth, conscience doesn't ask for permission. It just stings when you silence it.

Believing you can save everyone is nothing more than a self-centred delusion disguised as virtue.

The fantasy of saving everyone isn't rooted in compassion. It's rooted in control. It flatters the ego while pretending to serve others.

But people aren't broken puzzles waiting for your solution.

Some aren't meant to be saved. Some don't want to be. And some need to fall to see the ground for what it is.

The moment you believe your light is everyone's path, you've already wandered into shadow.

Expecting others to hinder you is how you justify staying distant. The wall you fear was never theirs to build.

This isn't caution, it's projection. We assign others the role of obstacle long before they ever move.

Why? Because it's easier to label people as threats than it is to risk being seen.

Distance becomes our excuse for not trusting, not connecting, not trying.

But the exile you fear from others begins with the prison you build for yourself.

We judge what we see, then spend the rest of the time justifying it as reason. That's what we label a first impression.

First impressions aren't shallow, they're just lazy.

We form them fast to feel in control, then spend the rest of the interaction looking for reasons to prove ourselves right.

It's not about seeing the truth in someone; it's about not wanting to be wrong.

In the end, most judgements say more about our fears than the person we're judging.

A smile is a crack in the mask. Even if it's small, it's still a vulnerability.

We've romanticised the smile as a gesture of warmth. But in truth, it's a glitch in the armour.

It reveals more than it hides. A smile says, "I acknowledge you", "I want something", or worse, "I'm not as guarded as I pretend to be".

That tiny break in emotional posture is a risk.

And in a world of performance, even a flicker of sincerity can be dangerous.

We come into the world fluent in deception. If anyone truly lived without a single lie, their life would be a fabrication in itself. Lying isn't the exception; it's the signature of being human.

We treat lies like cracks in a moral compass, but they're baked into the blueprint.

The first time a child hides pain, avoids punishment, or fakes a smile, they're learning survival, not sin.

The real danger isn't in lying. It's in pretending we don't.

The most dangerous people aren't those who deceive, they're the ones who believe they never do.

Give a person a mask, and it becomes a licence. Not to hide, but to act without consequence. What emerges is the face kept hidden beneath years of deliberate denial.

Anonymity doesn't conceal the truth; it accelerates its exposure.

Strip away the risk of judgement, and what surfaces isn't a better version of us.

It's the one we've spent years suppressing. The kind, composed, socially filtered self gives way to impulse, resentment, desire.

The mask doesn't create the monster. It just frees it from shame.

To know someone, is often just access to the fraction they've chosen to expose.

Most connections are illusions.

You don't see people. You see the curated feed of their personality, filtered through need, fear, and control.

What they show you isn't deception, it's protection. And sometimes, even they believe the version they've rehearsed.

So no, you don't know them. You've just been allowed into the showroom, not the factory.

Concealing stops feeling like performance the moment forgetting becomes easier than remembering.

What begins as concealment becomes habit. Not to deceive, but to endure.

You shape yourself to be palatable, to avoid rupture, to keep moving.

And slowly, the reasons dissolve, until all that remains is the role. Stripped of memory, but still intact.

You perform it so long, the original becomes irrelevant.

There's always a version of you that no one meets. Sometimes, not even you.

We wear the public face so often we forget it's not us. It's just the version that keeps everything functioning.

But beneath that utility is a self we haven't finished meeting. Not hidden from the world, but hidden from ourselves.

It's the part that aches without explanation, resents without reason, and sometimes sabotages what we say we want.

And if you never learn to look inward, you'll keep calling that stranger "fate."

The world prefers a persona it can explain. What you choose to show it, is the quiet rebellion.

Society doesn't demand conformity, it rewards it. It celebrates individuality in theory, then punishes what it can't label.

So, we shrink, round our edges, rehearse answers that fit into someone else's script.

But every time you refuse to simplify yourself for the comfort of others, that's rebellion.

It doesn't shout. It doesn't riot. It just exists, unapologetically.

II
COLLAPSE AND CONTROL

What bends doesn't always break.
Sometimes it hardens.

Perception sharpens us. Inspiration moves us. Reason keeps us from ruin. Lose one, and the rest unravel into delusion.

These aren't luxuries, they're core operating systems.

Perception shows you what's real. Inspiration gives you reason to act. Reason ensures you don't destroy everything along the way.

Society doesn't fall apart from a lack of rules. It crumbles when these three stop working in individuals.

Collapse doesn't always roar. Sometimes it begins with the quiet death of clarity.

A person who lacks self-control will obey anything stronger than their resolve, including their own weakness.

Discipline isn't about virtue, it's about survival.

Without it, you'll answer to whatever speaks the loudest: impulse, addiction, approval, fear.

Most people aren't controlled by tyrants; they're controlled by whatever emotion happens to rise first.

Self-control doesn't make you free. But without it, you'll never stop being ruled.

A person's greatest battle is internal. No enemy strikes deeper than the one who already knows their fear.

No enemy has better access than the one living in your head.

It doesn't need weapons, it has memories. It doesn't shout, it suggests. And it never needs to break you outright.

It just needs you to hesitate, to retreat, to believe the worst version of yourself.

That's how the inside wins. Quietly, and with your permission.

When endurance becomes identity, perseverance isn't strength. It's the performance of composure under threat.

The more you're praised for holding it together, the less permission you have to fall apart.

So, you adapt. You ritualise calm. You become fluent in silence.

And over time, composure becomes your cage. Not because it protects you, but because no one questions the version of you that never flinches.

That's not resilience. It's obedience in a mask.

*Growth begins the moment choice is made.
Quietly, and without applause.*

Change rarely begins with a breakthrough. It begins with a decision no one sees.

Not the kind you announce, but the kind that costs you something quietly.

No validation. No applause. Just you, choosing differently in a moment that didn't require it.

That's the threshold between intention and transformation. A small, silent rebellion against who you used to be.

You inherit the burden of effort, not the certainty of reward. And the burden has its price.

You're not promised anything. Not progress, not recognition, not success.

What you get is the right to try. That's it. You carry the weight because there's no other way forward.

And even if it breaks you, that doesn't make you special. It just makes you real.

Effort doesn't guarantee reward. It just proves you were willing to risk the silence.

A person who forgets history walks in circles, mistaking repetition for progress.

Repetition isn't always obvious. It disguises itself as movement, reinvention, even healing.

But patterns don't break on their own, they persist until you recognise the shape.

Forgetting history doesn't doom you to failure.

It just ensures you'll call it something else when it returns.

When justice becomes an obsession, it often recreates the very thing it set out to punish.

Justice turns to vengeance when it stops being about repair and starts being about satisfaction.

You convince yourself it's fairness, but what you want is impact. What you want is echo.

And by the time you deliver it, you're no longer correcting the wrong.

You're continuing it, with cleaner hands.

The world runs on imbalance. Some simply learn how to stand on the tilt.

The world doesn't fall short of fairness; it was never aiming for it.

Inequality isn't a glitch in the system. It's the logic it runs on.

Those who thrive aren't the most deserving. They're just the ones who stopped expecting the rules to be fair.

If you want balance, don't wait for it. Create it, or learn to walk without it.

Time doesn't heal. It just dulls the scream until silence feels familiar.

Healing is a myth we tell to make survival sound noble.

Time doesn't erase pain, it just buries it under routine, memory loss, and emotional scar tissue.

Eventually, you stop flinching. Not because it's gone, but because your mind learned how to carry it without crying out.

That's not healing. That's endurance.

Morality is a luxury of the untested. In the end, all that survives is the result.

Morality speaks loudest in comfort.

When survival enters the room, it goes quiet.

Pressure doesn't change who you are, it shows you what your values are worth when no one's watching.

In the end, history doesn't record virtue. It records outcomes.

Conviction doesn't vanish. It adapts until the shape of compromise starts passing for character.

Most people don't abandon what they believe. They just reshape it until it fits the environment that rewards their silence.

It starts as negotiation. Then adjustment. Then identity.

And by the time the trade becomes visible, it no longer feels like a trade, it feels like maturity. That's the danger of endurance in a broken system.

You survive by becoming what it needs from you. Then call the result integrity.

Equality may be an illusion, yet we find inequality difficult to reconcile with.

We understand inequality.

What we struggle with is accepting our place inside it.

It's not the concept that hurts. It's the way it makes you explain your losses while others inherit their wins.

The game doesn't hide its rules. It just counts on you hoping they'll change.

We evolve through action, not intent. Yet not all are measured the same. Still, we bind ourselves to the fantasy of equality in a world built on uneven ground.

We evolve through action, but not all actions weigh the same.

Some climb. Some get carried. And some are ignored no matter how loud they land.

We cling to the idea of merit because it makes failure feel fair.

But deep down, we know. The system doesn't reward effort. It rewards position.

Ease is a privilege of perspective. What you pass through effortlessly may be difficult for someone else to endure.

Struggle isn't always loud. And ease isn't always earned.

What's effortless for you might be survival for someone else.

We mistake our comfort for normal, then judge others for not matching it.

Empathy doesn't start with understanding. It starts with restraint.

III
TRUTH AS BLADE

The truth doesn't set you free.
It reveals what your cage is made of.

Truth doesn't wound once. It carves speaker and listener with the same blade.

Truth is rarely clean. It enters sharp but exits jagged, tearing something from both sides.

The speaker loses comfort, connection, maybe even love. The listener loses illusion.

But the real damage isn't in the words. It's in what they destroy silently: denial, identity, safety.

Truth doesn't care who bleeds. It just demands that someone does.

Everyone carries their own collapse. Some bury it in silence. Others learn to stand in its aftermath.

Collapse isn't always a breaking point; it's often a slow corrosion.

It eats at the edges; in moments no one sees. Some keep walking with the weight hidden behind a polished smile.

Others stumble openly and get labelled weak.

But the truth is, we all fracture. The only difference is how long we can pretend we haven't.

It's not the failure we fear. It's the echo of the judgement that follows after.

Failure ends. Judgement doesn't. The fall itself is private, sometimes even peaceful.

But once people know, it spreads. Stripped of nuance, distorted by retelling.

You become a story. A lesson. A joke. And worse, you start believing their version of you.

That's the cost of falling where others can see. Not the wound. The whisper that follows.

We chase knowledge as if it stays still. Unaware that truth, too, eventually slips from definition.

Truth isn't fixed, it's fleeting. What you swear by today may betray you tomorrow.

Certainty is a comfort, but knowledge is a tide. It pulls in and out, dragging your convictions with it.

And the tragedy isn't losing the truth.

It's still clinging to it after it's turned into something else entirely.

A mistake that is ignored is no longer a mistake. It's a decision.

The first time, it's an error. The second, it's a pattern. By the third, you've started defending it.

Mistakes only stay innocent when they're addressed. Leave them long enough, and they harden into belief.

That's how we rewrite guilt into habit, by pretending silence is neutral. It's not.

It's complicity in slow motion.

Desire often disguises itself as fulfilment. And that's how we come to embrace the hand that unravels us.

The things we chase don't always look like danger. Sometimes they wear comfort. Validation. Safety.

But if you look closely, you'll see the rot beneath the reward.

We don't walk into ruin blind. We walk in smiling, calling it love or purpose.

And by the time we realize we were wrong, we've already built a home out of our hunger.

What most call fate is merely consequence, too uncomfortable to claim as their own.

Fate is a lie we lean on when we don't want to be blamed.

It softens our reflection. It lets us reframe neglect as destiny, indecision as divine redirection.

But most of what breaks us wasn't written in the stars. It was written in the choices we kept avoiding.

Fate is just the name we give to our favourite excuse.

A person on the edge of genius is always one step from falling into madness.

Genius and madness share the same road.

One builds, the other burns. But both start with isolation, obsession, and the belief that you see what others can't.

The mind that elevates you can also unmake you.

And brilliance is never a guarantee; it's just a tighter wire to walk.

The roots of human error stem from two forces, haste and hesitation.

Every collapse starts with movement or its absence.

Some of us rush blindly, mistaking urgency for clarity. Others freeze, waiting for certainty that never arrives.

One creates damage. The other allows it. But both are masks for fear.

And fear, when unexamined, writes the script of every mistake we later pretend was accidental.

To believe everything or doubt everything, both absolve you of thought. Reflection is the only path that demands effort.

Blind belief is lazy. So is total cynicism.

One lets you sleep. The other lets you shrug. Neither demands you wrestle with truth.

But reflection? That's where the pain is. That's where growth hides.

It forces you to choose, to be wrong, to see yourself in the mess you'd rather blame on the world.

A person fails at life not by being wrong, but by mistaking another's path for their own.

You didn't fail because you lost.

You failed because you were chasing someone else's win. Their goals. Their timeline. Their definition of worth.

And in doing so, you slowly erased the parts of you that were never meant to fit that mould.

That's the worst kind of failure. The one that looks like success on paper.

Collapse doesn't come from the outside. It begins with the lies we start to believe. The most dangerous traitor lives behind your own intentions.

No betrayal cuts deeper than the one you deliver to yourself. Quietly, rationally, with good intentions.

You say you're being patient, careful, realistic.

But deep down, you know. You're stalling. You're shrinking.

And every excuse you tell yourself is just another rope tied around your own ankles.

What unsettles us most isn't the unknown. It's what we've already named, then dismissed.

We don't avoid truth because we can't see it.

We avoid it because seeing demands movement, and movement risks everything the lie keeps intact.

So, we nod quietly to what we already know, then resume the performance.

Not because we believe it. But because the alternative would require us to change what we've already decided to dismiss.

We condemn others for hiding the truth, but never question the truths we've buried out of convenience.

We demand transparency from others while living in curated denial.

We edit our flaws. We soften our failures. We avoid hard conversations with ourselves.

But the world doesn't mirror our truths, it mirrors our dishonesty. And the lies we hate in others?

They're just echoes of the ones we've made peace with.

What exposes us doesn't wait to be welcomed. It enters and breaks what silence made stable.

What exposes us doesn't arrive gently.

It interrupts. It indicts. It tears through timing. Not to enlighten, but to disrupt.

And those who carry it aren't treated as honest. They're treated as threats to the illusion that made everything seem stable.

That's the price of recognition. You don't get credit. You get blamed for shattering the script.

If truth is cruelty, then the lie becomes an act of care.

Not all truth is noble.

Sometimes we speak it to wound, not to reveal. And not all lies are poison. Sometimes they're mercy in disguise.

The line isn't between honesty and deception. It's between cruelty and intention.

And if you can't tell which one you're reaching for, then maybe it's both.

People escape inward reckoning through outward absurdity. The stranger the act, the deeper the denial.

Not all chaos is confusion. Sometimes it's design. Noise engineered to drown the quiet.

We escalate. We distort. We turn reality into theatre.

Not because we're lost, but because stillness might reveal what we've been rehearsing how to avoid.

It's easier to act strange than to sit with what's real. And most would rather perform than transform.

To believe something lasts forever is to watch its beauty fade.

Permanence is a comfort we cling to because we fear grief. But nothing beautiful survives being frozen.

We romanticize "forever" until it becomes repetition. Routine. Decay.

The more we try to keep something untouched, the faster it dulls. Love. Joy. Meaning.

They don't die from loss. They die from our refusal to let them change.

Truth doesn't sever connection. It strips away the illusion that made closeness feel safe.

Some bonds aren't built on truth. They're built on mutual avoidance, of the questions that would unravel the script.

You call it trust. You call it comfort. But what you really had was alignment. In silence, in denial, in fear of the truth.

And when it finally arrives, it doesn't shatter anything real.

It just reveals what only ever held when unexamined.

IV
POWER
WITHOUT NOISE

Silence is not absence.
It's intent without announcement.

There are lies of record and lies of promise. One distorts what was, the other delays what must be.

Some lies rewrite history. Others buy time from the future.

One edits what's already done. The other sells comfort on credit. But neither are accidents.

We don't lie because we're unsure. We lie because we're unwilling: to confront, to act, to let go.

The truth isn't too complex. It's too immediate. So, we stall with language until it's safe to pretend we never knew.

Time is the only currency that can't be forged, earned, or reclaimed.

You can steal money. Rebuild trust. Even borrow power. But time?

Once spent, it doesn't echo. It vanishes. It doesn't care what you traded it for. You don't get interest on regret. No refund for hesitation.

Every moment lost is final. That's why we avoid thinking about it.

Because deep down, we know we've been bleeding our life out by the second, and calling it preparation.

Even the strongest aren't immune. Alone, they learn to shatter in silence.

Strength doesn't break loudly, it erodes. It keeps showing up, keeps carrying, keeps performing.

Until one day it folds under the weight of everything it never said.

The strong don't collapse in public. They decay in solitude. And when they fall, it's not from weakness.

It's from being too reliable for too long, and never asking anyone to notice.

Those with ability rarely speak of it. Those without, rarely speak of anything else.

Power doesn't announce itself. It doesn't need to. The real ones don't seek credit, they seek outcome.

Meanwhile, the loud perform competence to hide insecurity. They narrate effort, inflate struggle, rehearse presence.

Because without results, all they have is volume.

But when you're built for it, the proof isn't in what you say. It's in what stops when you leave.

It takes greater skill to go unnoticed than it does to impress.

Visibility is easy. It just takes noise, timing, or a crowd. But influence without spotlight? That's mastery.

It's the move that shifts the room without taking centre stage.

The ones who impress are remembered. But the ones who go unnoticed?

They're the reason things work, break, or change. Silence is how true precision survives the performance.

Silence isn't weakness. Sometimes, it's the first move.

Loud actions beg for approval. Quiet ones get results.

Silence isn't absence, it's intent before impact. The loudest in the room are usually bluffing. But the quiet?

They've already decided. You just haven't seen the fallout yet.

Power doesn't argue. It lands.

Stillness, when honed, doesn't hold space. It occupies.

Stillness draws out whatever people bring into it. Some see calm. Others feel watched.

It becomes a mirror no one asked for. Quiet enough to reflect back every fear, every unfinished thought, every unspoken consequence.

That's why the most dangerous kind of presence doesn't move.

It waits.

What we call competition is often just deception dressed as merit.

Not every win is earned. Some are orchestrated. Some are handed over behind a smile.

Merit is a myth we cling to because it feels fair.

But in truth, the game rewards polish over principle. Charm over competence. Strategy over substance.

And if you think you're competing on skill alone, you've already been outplayed.

Control doesn't endure through presence. It survives through consequence.

Control doesn't need to raise its voice. It builds the walls, sets the terms, and vanishes.

What follows: the decisions, the silence, the caution. That's where it lives.

It survives in the hesitation before action; in the weight of rules no one remembers agreeing to.

Not through presence. But through outcome.

Life promises nothing. Only consequences, and the gamble required to reach them.

You don't earn outcomes; you wager on them.

Every step forward has a price, and life doesn't refund losses. It just keeps moving, asking more.

There are no guarantees. Only risks. You either stake your comfort, your image, your security. Or you stay stagnant and call it wisdom.

But stillness is a bet too. You just lose slower.

Victory isn't born from the avoidance of failure, but in how one endures its weight.

The win isn't in not falling. It's in standing back up without applause.

Pain is part of the path. Embarrassment. Doubt. Delay.

Most people break not because they lost, but because they couldn't carry the silence that followed.

Endurance is quiet. It bleeds inward. And it's the only real proof you meant it.

The harm of a friend who doesn't know better always outweighs the challenge of a rival who does.

You brace for enemies. You prepare for the opposition.

But it's the friendly fire that cuts deepest. The advice meant to help. The concern that limits. The loyalty that silences growth.

Enemies sharpen you. Friends dull you without meaning to.

And if you're not careful, the people who love you most will be the reason you stop evolving.

Not all restraint is discipline. Some wear it to be seen as harmless.

Not all performance needs motion. Some sit still. Deliberately, convincingly, and long enough for you to lower your guard.

Restraint can feel like safety, until you realise it's been managing your perception the whole time.

It doesn't speak. It doesn't need to.

It just positions itself, where suspicion won't reach.

IV
SURVIVAL
WITHOUT
APPLAUSE

Not all who endure survive clean.
Some survive in pieces.

You can name the sky and measure the light, but if you've never felt the core, all you've learned is the shape of your confinement.

Perspective isn't depth.

You can map the stars from your cell and still die never knowing what freedom feels like.

Insight without exposure is just a theory. Clever, but caged. People mistake knowing their limits for transcending them.

But if all you've mastered is the language of your walls, then your wisdom is just dressed-up confinement.

Everyone knows the world is far from perfect. Yet still, they fantasize of a place untouched by imperfection.

We don't dream of perfection because we expect it. We crave it because reality scrapes us raw.

Even when we know better, something inside us clings to the myth, that there's a place untouched by cruelty. Untouched by failure.

It's not logical. It's not even hopeful.

It's just the part of us that refuses to stop aching for something gentler than the truth.

Evil often begins where weakness is left unchecked.

Not all darkness starts with malice. Sometimes it begins with fear, silence, or the refusal to act.

We excuse failure, soften cowardice, and call inaction something noble like patience.

But rot spreads through what we allow, not what we confront.

And by the time you call it evil, it's already learned your voice.

No creature trades its nature. Only humans make bargains, and break them in silence.

Other creatures survive by instinct. Humans survive by illusion.

We create deals, expectations, and performances. Then break them behind polished words and polite smiles.

No animal negotiates its hunger. No wolf pleads fairness.

But we bargain away truth to feel civilized, then wonder why everything still feels feral underneath.

Being loved for who you're not hurts slower, but it cuts deeper than being hated for who you are.

Hatred is clean. It shows you the boundary. But being loved as someone you're not?

That's where erosion begins.

At first it feels safe, like acceptance. Then it starts to trap you in a version you never chose.

And the longer you wear it, the more you vanish. Smiling, approved, and slowly erased.

The most convincing lie carries just enough truth to slip past suspicion.

Lies don't need to be flawless. They just need to feel familiar.

The best ones echo something you already fear, or secretly want to believe. That's what makes them dangerous.

They don't confront you. They comfort you.

And by the time you see the damage, the lie is already part of your logic. Disguised as something you thought you chose.

Control your mind, and you'll survive what breaks most people. Including yourself.

Survival isn't strength. It's separation.

Most people collapse because they believe every voice in their head is real. But the ones who last? They listen without surrendering.

They still feel the storm, but they don't follow it. And that's what saves them. Not peace. Not freedom.

Just enough control to keep breathing when everything inside them wants to disappear.

There's no transformation without damage. Progress demands repayment. Quietly, painfully, and without warning.

Progress doesn't charge you at the start. It waits until you've changed, then sends the bill.

And by then, the damage is already woven in.

You lose time. You lose people. You lose parts of yourself you never planned to trade.

The shift is real, but the cost compounds quietly. And the further you go, the less of you returns.

Some inherit ease. Others exhaust themselves chasing what was handed away without effort.

The world doesn't deal in fairness.

Some are born into comfort, into shortcuts, into doors already open. Others grind for scraps, just to taste what someone else calls normal.

It's not merit that separates them. It's inheritance. And pretending otherwise only deepens the bruise.

Because the hardest truth isn't that life is unfair. It's that some people never have to notice.

Darkness doesn't repel, it seeks itself. And in time, the stronger shadow always consumes the weaker.

Darkness doesn't chase light. It finds more of itself.

The broken recognize each other, even if they don't speak. What draws them together isn't healing. It's hunger.

When two shadows meet, it's never equal. One consumes. The other surrenders.

And by the time you notice which one you've become, it's already too late to pull yourself back out.

Everyone's built from both strength and weakness. What makes us human is how well we hide the second one.

Being human isn't about balance. It's about disguise.

We don't survive by embracing weakness, we survive by masking it. A joke. A distraction. A smile timed just right.

People think composure means control.

But often, it just means the collapse has been delayed.

We're born fragile, overflowing with potential. But survival teaches us to endure, not to grow.

We enter the world unfinished, dependent, open, unprotected.

The world answers that openness with pressure. Not guidance. Not wisdom.

Just the slow grind of fear, rejection, and expectation. So, we adapt. Not by rising, but by armouring.

We don't grow into who we were meant to be. We shrink into who we need to be to stay alive.

Trauma doesn't respond to words. It answers only to memory.

You can name the wound. You can even rationalize it. But your body remembers in silence.

It reacts without asking. Flinches before thought. Because trauma doesn't respond to explanations, it reacts to echoes.

It doesn't live in language. It lives in repetition. And healing doesn't mean forgetting.

It means learning how to survive the return.

Worry sharpens the mind just enough to miss what matters.

Worry doesn't prepare you. It distracts you. It feels like focus, but it's fixation.

You obsess over what might go wrong, and miss the thing already slipping away.

That's how worry works. It drains your presence while convincing you that you're alert.

And by the time the real moment comes, it's already behind you.

Tears don't fall for what's lost. They fall for the silence that confirms no one is coming.

We don't cry from pain. We cry when we realize no one's coming.

The waiting. The silence. The slow realization that help isn't on its way. That's when it breaks you.

Not the pain itself, but the loneliness wrapped around it.

Tears don't mourn pain. They mourn hope that overstayed.

Fear fades not from strength, but from overexposure. Enough pain, and even terror forgets how to feel.

Fear doesn't vanish; it starves. And when it returns, it doesn't knock.

You don't grow out of it; you burn through it. Pain stops feeling sharp. Misery stops feeling loud.

Eventually, fear stops arriving at all. Not because it respects you, but because it knows there's nothing left to shake.

That isn't peace. It's what's left when even panic gives up.

What breaks in silence never earns sympathy. It's erosion without spectacle that goes unseen.

Not every wound asks for attention. Some just settle beneath the surface, wearing you down in increments too small to notice.

You keep functioning. You keep speaking. You keep showing up.

And when nothing falls apart, they assume nothing's wrong.

That's the price of surviving well. You disappear into what held.

You didn't find answers.
You found reflection.

www.ingramcontent.com/pod-product-compliance
Lightning Source LLC
Chambersburg PA
CBHW060409080526
44583CB00012B/513